NORTH AMERICAN NATURAL RESOURCES

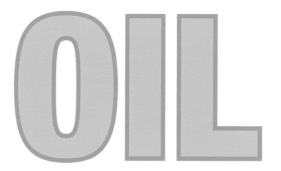

North American Natural Resources

Coal

Copper

Freshwater Resources

Gold and Silver

Iron

Marine Resources

Natural Gas

Oil

Renewable Energy

Salt

Timber and Forest Products

Uranium

NORTH AMERICAN
NATURAL RESOURCES

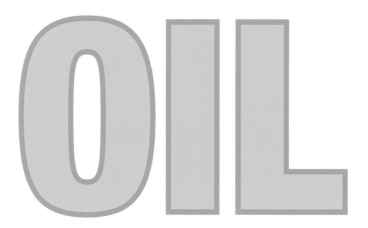

OIL

Steve Parker

MASON CREST

Mason Crest
450 Parkway Drive, Suite D
Broomall, PA 19008
www.masoncrest.com

MTM Publishing, Inc.
435 West 23rd Street, #8C
New York, NY 10011
www.mtmpublishing.com

President: Valerie Tomaselli
Vice President, Book Development: Hilary Poole
Designer: Annemarie Redmond
Illustrator: Richard Garratt
Copyeditor: Peter Jaskowiak
Editorial Assistant: Andrea St. Aubin

Series ISBN: 978-1-4222-3378-8
ISBN: 978-1-4222-3386-3
Ebook ISBN: 978-1-4222-8560-2

Library of Congress Cataloging-in-Publication Data
Parker, Steve, 1952-
  Oil / by Steve Parker.
    pages cm. — (North American natural resources)
  ISBN 978-1-4222-3386-3 (hardback) — ISBN 978-1-4222-3378-8 (series) —
ISBN 978-1-4222-8560-2 (ebook)
 1. Petroleum engineering—Juvenile literature. 2. Petroleum reserves—
North America—Juvenile literature. I. Title.
  TN870.3.P369 2015
  338.2'7282—dc23
                        2015005878

Printed and bound in the United States of America.

First printing
9 8 7 6 5 4 3 2 1

TABLE OF CONTENTS

Key Icons to Look for:

 Words to Understand: These words with their easy-to-understand definitions will increase the reader's understanding of the text, while building vocabulary skills.

 Sidebars: This boxed material within the main text allows readers to build knowledge, gain insights, explore possibilities, and broaden their perspectives by weaving together additional information to provide realistic and holistic perspectives.

 Research Projects: Readers are pointed toward areas of further inquiry connected to each chapter. Suggestions are provided for projects that encourage deeper research and analysis.

 Text-Dependent Questions: These questions send the reader back to the text for more careful attention to the evidence presented there.

 Series Glossary of Key Terms: This back-of-the-book glossary contains terminology used throughout the series. Words found here increase the reader's ability to read and comprehend higher-level books and articles in this field.

Note to Educator: As publishers, we feel it's our role to give young adults the tools they need to thrive in a global society. To encourage a more worldly perspective, this book contains both imperial and metric measurements as well as references to a wider global context. We hope to expose the readers to the most common conversions they will come across outside of North America.

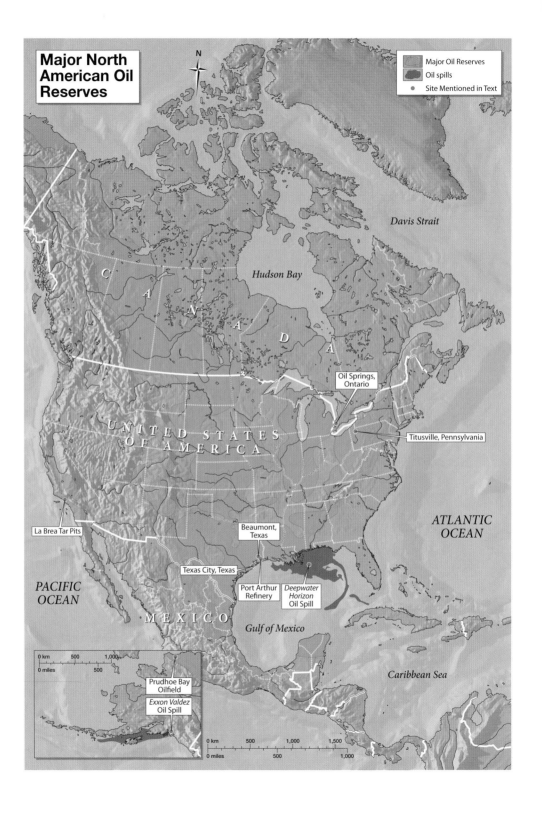

Major North American Oil Reserves

Major Oil Reserves
Oil spills
Site Mentioned in Text

N

Davis Strait

C A N A D A

Hudson Bay

Oil Springs, Ontario

UNITED STATES OF AMERICA

Titusville, Pennsylvania

ATLANTIC OCEAN

La Brea Tar Pits

Beaumont, Texas

PACIFIC OCEAN

Texas City, Texas

Port Arthur Refinery

Deepwater Horizon Oil Spill

M E X I C O

Gulf of Mexico

Caribbean Sea

0 km   500   1,000
0 miles   500

Prudhoe Bay Oilfield

Exxon Valdez Oil Spill

0 km   500   1,000   1,500
0 miles   500   1,000

INTRODUCTION

Oil is one of the world's most needed resources. Whenever we ride in a car, take a plane, use electricity, handle plastic, brush paint, apply wax, varnish nails, or even step onto a sidewalk, oil and its by-products are probably involved.

Why has oil become so important in modern life? One reason is that oil is not just one single substance. It's a complicated mixture of many different ingredients, formed over millions of years from the long-dead remains of ancient life forms. Today, oil can be taken from under the ground and turned into hundreds of useful products by the processes

Oil pumps like these are sometimes called "nodding donkeys." (Elena Elisseeva/Dreamstime)

of heat, cooling, and chemicals. It is also a wonderful energy source: It is burned in fires, furnaces, and power generators, and it is exploded as gasoline and diesel in motors, or as kerosene in jet engines.

Even oil's liquid nature helps make it useful, since it is so moveable. Unlike rival energy sources like coal, or raw materials like metal-containing rock ores, oil flows. It oozes along tubes from wells into giant supertankers and through pipelines thousands of miles long.

In recent years, fuel products from oil—chiefly gasoline, diesel, kerosene, and heating oils—have provided about 35 percent of all energy consumed in North America. This compares to 27 percent for natural gas, 19 percent for coal, and 10 percent for renewable sources such as hydroelectric, wind, and solar. Of the energy from oil, by far the largest amount—over 70 percent—drives automobiles, airplanes, ships, and other transportation. Another 25 percent is consumed by general industry, while only 1 percent generates electric power.

Oil is among the most useful substances in the world. But problems come with its use, including pollution, disasters, and long-term harm to the environment, such as climate change. Although oil use is declining somewhat in North America, demand for the resource is expanding in developing areas of the world, such as East Asia, South Asia, and South America. Crises in oil supply and demand have led to labor strikes, riots, and even wars.

Oil touches almost every part of our daily lives. It is one of North America's greatest resources and an essential part of industry and business. Yet it is also a source of many difficulties. Oil is so many things—precious, valuable, adaptable, and even essential, but also problematic and limited.

Chapter One

HOW OIL FORMED

When you picture oil, you probably imagine a dark, thick, and gloppy substance. And oil can indeed look this way. But crude oil varies in its appearance. Depending on how it formed, and on the amounts of its various substances, it may be thin and runny, or it may be thick like molasses. It also varies in color from light brown to almost black. Despite these different forms, nearly all oil begins in the same way.

Words to Understand

hydrocarbon: a substance containing only the pure chemical substances, or elements, carbon and hydrogen.

kerogens: a variety of substances formed when once-living things decayed and broke down, on the way to becoming oil.

petroleum: meaning "rock oil," a natural liquid substance formed over a very long time within the Earth, from the remains of once-living things.

porous: allowing a liquid to seep or soak through small holes and channels.

Death, Pressure, and Temperature

For hundreds of millions of years, tiny living things thrived in oceans, seas, and lakes. They would be too small to see except through a microscope. Similar living things are in our lakes, seas, and oceans today. They go under the general name of plankton, meaning "drifters."

Some of these living things, known as *protists*, were similar to microscopic plants. They trapped light energy from the sun by a process called photosynthesis (building with light) to power their life processes. They took in raw materials and minerals from the water around them in order to grow. They were known as *phytoplankton*. Other kinds of protists, also microscopic, were called *zooplankton*. Like animals, they consumed food for energy and nourishment—by feeding on the phytoplankton or on each other.

Over millions of years, countless billions of these life forms thrived and died. Their remains settled on the bottoms of seas and lakebeds, along with other bits and pieces such as dead fish, shellfish, and seaweeds, and broken-off, worn-down particles of rocks, like sand and mud. Under certain conditions, generally when the water was warm and rich in nutrients, these remains were so plentiful that decay or rotting away could not happen fast enough. Instead, the remains began to collect and pile up in layers of ooze on the seabed.

Slowly the layers got deeper. The weight of the upper ones pressed down the lower, squashing them at high pressure. This high pressure in turn made the temperature of the layers rise. The increase in pressure and temperature caused the remains of the once-living microplants and microcreatures to cook and break down. They became waxy, slimy substances called kerogens, and mixed with

Plankton

Living things that drift in the water, rather than actively swimming where they want, are known as *plankton*. There are microscopic plant-like phytoplankton, and microscopic animal-like zooplankton. There are also the eggs and tiny young of large creatures such as fish, crabs, shellfish, and starfish. Some plankton is quite large—for example, jellyfish are considered plankton because of their drifting.

These sandstone rock layers in Utah took millions of years to create.

the rocky particles that had also settled on the seabed. In effect, those original living things were gradually preserved as fossils—like the bones and teeth of dinosaurs and other prehistoric creatures.

Motor oil is used to reduce friction in car engines. It needs to be changed regularly because dirt can build up and prevent the oil from working well.

Kerogens contain mainly the chemical substances known as **hydrocarbons**. These are chemicals composed of only the elements (pure substances) carbon (symbol C) and hydrogen (symbol H).

Millions more years passed. In some places, the settled layers were buried even deeper. At temperatures of around 120 to 300°F (50 to 150°C), usually a depth of 1 to 2 miles (1.6 to 3.2 kilometers) below the surface, the kerogens broke down further. They gradually changed into what we call crude oil or **petroleum**. Like kerogens, the oil—and natural gas, formed in much the same way—contained mostly hydrocarbons. This is why now they are sometimes known as hydrocarbon fuels or hydrocarbon materials. Another name for oil or the fuels made from it is *fossil fuels*, since they formed by the process known as fossilization. Yet another term is *organic materials*, or *organic fuels*, which means they are connected to living things and nature, rather than being man-made or artificial.

This process took immense lengths of time and occurred only in certain places around the world. It depended on the right conditions coming together, from the layers of dead sea-life forming in the first place, to deeper burial, and high pressures and temperatures. Also needed were suitable kinds of rocks. Some were **porous**, with tiny holes and channels like a sponge. This allowed oil to collect in them, in the same way that a sponge holds water. The oil might seep or travel for hundreds of miles when doing this.

The main kinds of oil-bearing porous rocks were sandstone and a type of limestone known as "coarse grained," due to its relatively large particles, or grains. These rocks were hard, not soft like a sponge, but they did have very tiny holes and cavities, which the oil filled. The oil was kept here by other kinds of rocks around them, which were nonporous and prevented the oil from oozing away.

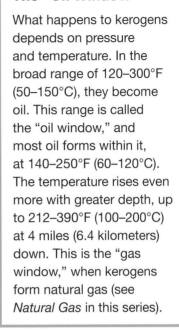

The "Oil Window"

What happens to kerogens depends on pressure and temperature. In the broad range of 120–300°F (50–150°C), they become oil. This range is called the "oil window," and most oil forms within it, at 140–250°F (60–120°C). The temperature rises even more with greater depth, up to 212–390°F (100–200°C) at 4 miles (6.4 kilometers) down. This is the "gas window," when kerogens form natural gas (see *Natural Gas* in this series).

An oil rig in the Gulf of Mexico pulls oil up from beneath the sea floor.

Where Oil Formed

As all these processes happened, the slowly forming oil eventually collected inside the porous rocks in huge underground formations known as oil traps. (Oil is not found in enormous underground pools or lakes, as some people think; it is always in porous rocks.)

The continent of North America was one major place where kerogen, oil formation, and oil traps occurred. Long ago, seas and oceans covered much of what is now dry land. In certain regions, including the northwestern and southeastern parts of North America, the conditions were right for plentiful oil formation. The Gulf of Mexico also had suitable conditions. Elsewhere in the world, main regions of oil formation include the Middle East and parts of Russia.

Over time, great earth movements tilted or shifted the oil reserves. Continents drifted, pushing up mountains, while earthquakes split the ground. So today, some oil is near the surface. It may even ooze up and out, onto the ground, forming natural

Oil at the Surface

In some places, oil and tar ooze onto the surface. This happened at the La Brea Tar Pits in Los Angeles, California, beginning about 40,000 years ago. Leaves, twigs, and other bits covered the surface. When animals walked here, they were trapped in the sticky mess; many of them died and were preserved by the tar. The La Brea site includes mammoths, saber-toothed cats, wolves, bears, and ground sloths.

The La Brea Tar Pits in Los Angeles, California, is one of America's most famous fossil sites. The park now has statues to show what it might have been like for the prehistoric animals who passed by.

Dinosaurs and Oil

You might have heard someone say that oil comes "from dinosaurs," but this is a myth. As we've noted here, oil deposits develop from the remains of microscopic living things, not from larger animals, or even from bigger plants.

pools. In other places, the oil is very deep, far under the surface of the land or the seabed.

Oil has probably been forming in the earth for more than 1,000 million years. The oil we use today was mainly formed from 200 million to 10 million years ago. Nine-tenths of North America's known oil reserves date to this time span. It covers the prehistoric periods of the Jurassic (201–145 million years ago), Cretaceous (145–66 million), Paleogene (66–23 million), and Neogene (23–2.5 million) periods. While dinosaurs roamed the land during the Jurassic and the Cretaceous periods, microscopic life forms were dying in seas, oceans, and lakes, on their way to becoming oil.

The process of oil formation still continues, but at a much-reduced rate, because conditions in seas and lakes are less suitable compared to millions of years ago. In any case, oil formation takes millions of years to complete. The result: ancient oil is being used up millions of times faster than it could ever form today.

TEXT-DEPENDENT QUESTIONS

1. What kinds of living things were involved in the formation of oil?
2. Which types of rocks are best at holding oil?
3. Why did oil form in some parts of the world but not others?

RESEARCH PROJECTS

1. Find out about the Western Interior Seaway (also called the Cretaceous Seaway or the North American Inland Sea). How was it involved in oil formation?
2. How do the oil window temperatures necessary for the formation of oil compare with other high temperatures, like those in a domestic cooker, pottery kiln, barbeque, or steel-making furnace?

Chapter Two

EXTRACTING OIL

Words to Understand

bit: the hard-toothed tip of the oil drill that turns to grind its way through rock.

blowout: a sudden, uncontrolled gush of oil (or gas) from a borehole or established well.

fracking: shorthand for hydraulic fracturing, a method of extracting gas and oil from rocks.

refine: to remove impurities from something.

remote sensing: detecting and gathering information from a distance, such as when satellites in space measure the air and ground temperature below.

For thousands of years, around the world, people used oil and similar natural liquids in many ways. They burned it for light, heat, and cooking. They painted it onto ships, tents, roofs, urns, buckets, and many other surfaces for waterproofing. They smeared it onto skin rashes and other skin problems of both people and animals. They used thin oil's slippery nature to lubricate cart wheels and early machines. They laid thick tar onto tracks to make smooth surfaces.

Some of this oil came from natural pools and pits on or just beneath the surface. It was simply scooped up or collected as it oozed out of the dirt. More than 1,500 years ago, people in China used hard metal- or stone-tipped wooden drills to bore down dozens of feet beneath the surface, and they would then gather the oil that oozed up the hole. In 1273, the great Italian traveler Marco Polo, while journeying through Asia's present-day Georgia and Azerbaijan, described how large amounts of oil were obtained by scooping or digging, and then taken away in ships. But methods of extracting oil—getting it out of the ground—remained small-scale and simple.

In the 1840s, chemists in Europe and then North America discovered how to treat various kinds of natural oil to make a liquid that burned well in lamps. They quickly found out how to get this liquid from coal, which was mined as a popular fuel at the time, and from other rocks, like shale. Demand for this lamp oil—similar to today's kerosene—grew fast, but supplies were limited.

The caravan of Marco Polo, depicted by the mapmaker Abraham Cresques in 1375.

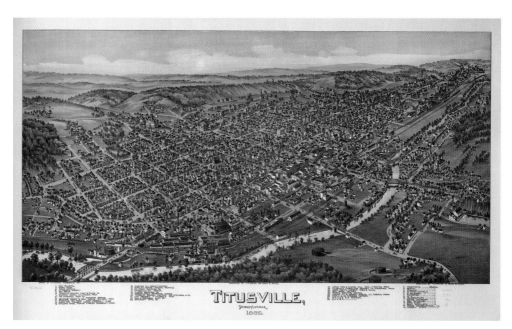

A map of Titusville, Pennsylvania, in 1896. Between 1860, just months after the oil strike, and 1870, Titusville experienced a population growth rate of almost 2,000 percent.

Two advances in the late 1850s, both in North America, sparked the modern oil business. In 1858 at Black Creek, Ontario, Canada, the businessman James Miller Williams drilled a water well but found oil instead. It was soon being **refined** into various products, including lamp oil. The "oil rush" town of Black Creek grew fast, even changing its name to Oil Springs.

The next year, 1859, a former railroad conductor named Edwin Drake drilled a well at Titusville, Pennsylvania. He had been employed by Seneca Oil to explore around natural surface oil seeps. After weeks of slow progress drilling to a depth of 69 feet (21 meters), Drake at last struck oil. It was a turning point. Knowledge about drilling spread rapidly and a commercial oil boom began.

Drake did not invent drilling for underground resources. Instead, he adapted methods already in use to find water, salt, and other minerals. He did not use a rotating drill but a percussive one, where a chisel-like tip banged down to chip away the rock. But he did put together improved equipment and methods, such as using steam engines to power the drill, and inserting a tube-like lining in the deepening hole to stop it from collapsing.

Looking for Oil

Geologists are central to the search for oil, because they are experts in the rocks and soils that make up the Earth. In surface surveys, they look for certain kinds of features, such as hills, valleys, and particular types of rocks and soil, which often occur over oil traps and oil-bearing rocks. They may drive or walk across an area and take samples. They also fly over in aircraft, and they look at different types of **remote-sensing** satellite photographs taken from space. When seeking oil beneath the seabed, divers or remote-controlled submersible crafts make surveys and take samples.

The geologists and surveyors use a variety of measuring devices. The gravimeter (short for "gravity meter") detects tiny differences in Earth's downward pull of gravity. Heavy, dense rocks in an area increase gravity very slightly, while lighter, oil-bearing rocks reduce it. Another device is the magnetometer, which senses any minute changes in Earth's natural magnetic field, which again is affected by oil-bearing rocks below. There are also electronic machines called sniffers that respond to the faintest scent of oil wafting into the air.

Another hugely important method is seismic studies. Seismic waves are vibrations or "shaking" that pass through Earth's rocks, soils, and other structures—seen in their most powerful form in earthquakes. Seismic surveys involve creating "mini-earthquakes" and measuring how far and fast the waves or vibrations travel through the ground or seabed. The vibrations are picked up at various distances by sensors known as seismometers, enabling scientists to figure out whether the rocks contain any oil.

The results from all these tests are studied carefully. The geologists and oil experts discuss how much oil there might be, how deep it is, and how easy it could be to extract. They might then decide on the next stage: to drill.

Roughnecks

Oil drilling can be tough work, and workers on rigs are often known as "roughnecks." This name dates from the days of travelling fairgrounds and carnivals in the 19th century. And it was used even before that, for people who tended to do hard manual work, act tough, and get into fights. Although it was originally an insult, roughneck is often a term of pride among people who work on rigs.

A drill pipe.

Drilling for Oil

Before drilling, the oil company makes sure it has legal permission to drill in a particular area of land or sea—that is, onshore or offshore. Onshore, a drill rig and camp are set up—which may mean trucking or even helicoptering machinery into remote areas like the icy wilds of Alaska. Offshore, as in the Gulf of Mexico, the company arranges for drilling rigs or ships and supply vessels.

A drill consists of a very tough rotating tip with grinding teeth, called the **bit**, that sits on the end of a long hollow pipe. The pipe spins and bores its way into the rock. The bit is made from the hardest metals and perhaps a coating of tiny, even harder, diamonds. Some bits simply turn and scrape the rock, while others also make vibrations that shatter it. At the drill rig, the bit and pipe hang inside a tall girder tower that can hoist them out of the ground, called a *derrick*. They are turned by a circular rotary table or turntable around the pipe, driven by powerful motors. This grips a special upper part of the pipe with flat sides or ridges, called the *kelly*.

Close-up view of a bit for oil drilling.

As the drill bit goes down into the rock, more lengths of pipe—usually 31 feet (9.5 meters), or perhaps longer—are screwed onto the top end. This continues, deeper and deeper, with dozens or hundreds of pipes all screwed together end to end, called the

A Big Industry

Almost everything about the oil industry is *big*—especially giant offshore oil rigs and platforms. Some sit on long legs resting on the ocean floor. Others float, kept in position by long chains and cables fixed to weights on the seabed. The largest platforms weigh over 200,000 tons (181,000 metric tons) and stand 2,000 feet (610 meters) above the seabed. Some tower more than 350 feet (107 meters) above the waves. Drilling ships can bore holes in water 10,000 feet (3048 meters) deep.

Also on the ocean, oil-carrying supertankers are the largest vessels afloat. They are called ULCCs or Ultra Large Crude Carriers. Some reach 1,500 feet (457 meters) long and 220 feet (67 meters) wide. Such massive size lowers the cost of oil transport. However, their size is limited on some routes by shallow water, bridges or canals.

The *SSCV Thialf*, a semi-submersible crane vessel, at the Perdido oil drilling platform in the Gulf of Mexico. The Perdido platform, left, sits over the deepest oil well in the world.

drill string. The width of the hole, or bore, depends on the drill bit size and may be anything from a few inches to over 3 feet. Usually it gets narrower in stages as it goes down. The borehole's depth varies with the location of the oil-bearing rocks, from a few hundred feet to many thousands. On land, the deepest boreholes go down over 6 miles, and under the seabed, more than 2 miles.

The incredible forces and friction on the drill bit would make it overheat and wear out fast. So a water-based liquid called drilling fluid—or "mud"—is pumped down inside the hollow drill string and out through the bit. Here it lubricates and cools the bit as it eats away the rock. The mud then flows back up around the drill string to the surface, to be filtered and reused. Different kinds of mud contain air bubbles, clay or similar particles, perhaps oil, and chemicals such as acids. Examining the mud as it comes to the surface shows the kind of rock below—and whether there is oil.

As the borehole deepens, it is lined by sections of tubes called casings, made of concrete or steel. They stop the sides of the hole from collapsing and keep the mud flowing. More borehole is drilled, the drill string lengthens, and more casings are added. Oil workers check the progress of the drill by taking samples and measurements. The drilling process is especially difficult offshore, due to fierce winds, high waves, and storms.

Deep underground, oil deposits are under enormous pressure. When the borehole punctures the deposit, the pressure can send the oil spurting upward, causing a **blowout,** or "gusher." Blowouts can be stopped by special seals called *blowout preventers* around the drill string.

Directional Drilling and Fracking

As a drill bit spins, it usually makes a straight borehole, although it may be pushed slightly off course by exceptionally hard rocks. Depending on the results of early exploratory boreholes, the same rig might then drill more boreholes from the same surface place, but at different angles into and through the ground. In horizontal or steerable drilling, the angle of the drill bit can be changed slightly so that the borehole, rather than going straight, curves or bends. Eventually the hole might

Workers pose with the head of a fracking pump in North Dakota.

curve from vertical to horizontal, or sideways, running parallel with the surface
for miles. These various methods can send boreholes along inside a widespread
reservoir of oil to reach a much greater area, rather than simply drilling down into
one part of it. They can also also reach oilfields where drilling from above would be
a problem, such as under towns or national parks.

Eventually the main drilling is finished. The drill string is then removed, and the bore is fitted with various kinds of tubes to bring out the oil. At the surface, the upper end of the hole is made safe, or capped, and fitted with a set of tubes, valves, meters and lights—referred to as a "Christmas tree"—to control the oil's flow. At the lower end, chemicals are pumped in to dissolve or crack the rocks around the casings and let the oil flow.

The traditional type of oil well described above was pioneered in North America, as were most of the improvements in technology. Since the 1950s, also beginning in North America, a method called hydraulic fracturing—**fracking** for short—has increased. It is used to extract oil and gas from rocks such as shale, where these resources are held tightly in very tiny pores. The pores are too small, and perhaps not joined together enough, to allow the oil or gas to flow out easily. So a well is drilled and then fluid is pumped down it, into the rocks, at incredibly high pressure. The pressurized fluid forces its way into the rocks and makes tiny holes, cracks and fractures that allow the oil or gas to flow.

Horizontal drilling and fracking allow oil and gas companies to access these resources where they were formerly impossible to extract. It also brings new life to old wells, yielding fresh supplies of oil and gas after the usual methods of extraction run dry.

Production and Transport

The drill site now becomes a production site. Tilting-arm pumps called pumpjacks or "nodding donkeys" may suck up the oil if there is not enough pressure below. The oil flows along pipes to a central location at the oilfield. If the region is rich in oil, a refinery may be built nearby, as explained in the next chapter. If not, the oil is sent along oil pipelines, in tanker trucks, or in waterway barges to a refinery farther away. It could also be piped to a transport center, usually a port, where it flows into the world's biggest ships, known as supertankers. Here it begins its journey to refineries that can be halfway around the world.

A pumpjack or "nodding donkey" creates pressure that helps pull oil into the pipes.

TEXT-DEPENDENT QUESTIONS

1. What are seismic studies?
2. On a drill platform, what is "mud" used for?
3. When drilling for oil, what is a Christmas tree?

RESEARCH PROJECTS

1. Research the history of fracking. When and where did it start? More recently, when did it suddenly start to become so popular, especially in North America?
2. Find out about oil pipelines in North America. Look for the longest, the widest, and those with the biggest flow. How is the oil kept moving, and what precautions are taken to prevent leaks and damage?

Chapter Three

OIL INTO PRODUCTS

O il or petroleum straight from nature is "crude" in the sense that it is original and untreated—that is, it's raw oil. The next main task is to process or treat the oil, separating its many different substances or ingredients. This is known as *refining* oil.

Not all crude oil is the same. Petroleum chemists need to know the features of each batch, since it affects which products it will yield. So, crude is measured and described in various ways. Many of these first came from North America, where the modern oil industry began.

Measurements of Oil

One common measure is API gravity. API is the acronym for the American Petroleum Institute, and gravity refers to weight. More accurately, it is density—the mass (weight) of a certain volume of oil, at a standard temperature of 60°F (15°C),

Workers fill an oil barrel at Dingman well, in Alberta, Canada, in 1914.

and at a standard pressure. Water is understood to have 10 degrees of API gravity. Numbers higher than 10 indicate that the substance is less heavy or less dense than water. In general terms:

- **Light crude** is usually more than 37 degrees API (32 for oil not produced in the United States).
- **Medium crude** is between 37 (or 32) and 22.
- **Heavy crude** is below 22.
- **Extra-heavy crude** is below 10.

Another measure of crude oil is the amount of sulfur it contains. This has a big effect on how to treat and refine it, and on which products will result. The two terms here are *sweet* and *sour*. Sweet crude oil generally has a sulfur content of less than 0.5 percent (less than 1/200th), while sour crude oil has a sulfur content greater than 0.5 percent.

As an example, one of the main kinds of crude oil is West Texas Intermediate (WTI), also called "Texas light sweet." It is a "benchmark" crude, meaning that it is used as a worldwide standard, or average, in the oil business. Its features are a light API gravity of about 39–40 degrees and a sweet sulfur content of 0.25–0.3 percent. Another standard type is Brent crude from Europe's North Sea, which has a slightly heavier API of 38 and is slightly less sweet at 0.35–0.4 percent sulfur.

A further measure that came from the pioneering North American oilfields in Pennsylvania is barrels. This refers to the volume of crude oil and its products. Of course, oil is no longer transported in wooden barrels by wagon and railroad, but the name has stuck. One standard barrel is 42 US gallons (almost 35 imperial gallons, or 159 liters). Very approximately, it would fill one and a half bathtubs. The amounts of reserves in oilfields are usually measured in barrels, as are the amounts extracted and refined. As an example, the Prudhoe Bay oilfield in North Alaska, North America's largest, once contained an estimated 24 billion barrels. Around the year 2000, it was producing 300,000 barrels daily, although that has since been reduced. After refining, one barrel of light crude produces around half its volume of gasoline, along with other fuels like heating oil, and other products.

From boots and jeans to sunglasses and umbrellas, the fashion industry depends on petroleum products.

Fractions of Oil

How is crude oil split into its many components or ingredients? The key is heat. Compared to liquids like water, oils are relatively **volatile**: when heated, they turn more easily from liquid into vapor or gas. Crude oil is a complex mixture of dozens, or even hundreds, of different volatile substances. When it is heated gradually (not burned), the substances in it vaporize at different temperatures. First are those with the smallest and lightest tiny particles, or molecules. Their vapor floats away. With increasing temperature, other substances do the same, one by one, each with larger molecules. Eventually, what remains are thick, tarry substances with big, heavy molecules that need very high temperatures to vaporize.

Distilleries

Distilling is an age-old method to separate and purify liquids. It is still very important in many industries. One of its earliest uses was to make alcoholic spirit drinks like whiskey and gin. Distilling crude oil was an evolution of this ancient method.

Each kind of vapor can be collected, cooled, and **condensed**—a process that changes it back into liquid form. Doing this for each vapor in turn produces a series of pure liquids from the original crude mixture. The oil has now been purified or refined into its separate ingredients, which are called *fractions* because they are parts of a whole. The general process of heating and vaporizing a liquid, and then cooling and condensing it, is known as **distillation**. So the whole method is known as fractional distillation.

At the Refinery

A typical oil refinery is a like a giant distillation plant with miles of pipes and tubes, dozens of tall towers, and hundreds of taps, valves, dials, and controls. The crude oil is heated in or next to the base of a tall cylinder-shaped tower, which is called the distillation tower or fractionation column. This tower is hottest at the bottom and coolest at the top. The crude oil vaporizes into its various fractions inside. The lightest fraction rises to the top of the tower, which may be over 200 feet high. Here the temperature is right for the vapor to cool, condense into liquid, collect in shallow

Aerial view of an oil refinery in Texas.

trays, and flow away along a pipe. The next heaviest fraction does the same but slightly lower down, where it is warmer, and so on, all the way down the tower.

The crude oil itself is heated to over 1,100°F (600°C) and its vapors rise up the tower as follows:

- At the top of the tower it might only be 70–120°F (20–50°C). Gases are led away here, such as methane, ethane, propane, and butane. These burn well as fuels, and are also used to make plastics.
- The next level down is around 120–175°F (50–80°C). Collected here ae substances called naphthas, ligroins, and petroleum ethers, which are used by the chemical industry.

Oil Cities

Oil refineries are so huge, they are like small cities. Hundreds of people work among the maze of tanks, towers, tubes, and other equipment. The first refineries, in the 1880s in Pennsylvania, processed 10 barrels of crude oil each day. The biggest in North America today is Port Arthur Refinery on the Gulf Coast in eastern Texas, handling half a million barrels daily.

A jet plane burns around 1 gallon of fuel (roughly 4 liters) per second when in the air. According to the US Energy Information Administration, airlines consumed an average of 1.4 million barrels of jet fuel per day in 2013. That's a lot, but it's actually down from previous years. In 2000, the average was 1.7 million barrels per day.

- Below this, at 140–300°F (60–150°C), is the motor fuel gasoline, or petrol.
- Farther down, in the temperature range 340–480°F (170–250°C), is the level for kerosene fuel. This is used in jet engines, some boat and heavy vehicle engines, certain kinds of rockets, and lamps and ovens. It is also used to make other petroleum products.
- Next come fuels such as diesel and light heating oil. The temperature range here is 410–570°F (210–300°C).
- Below this is the level for lubricating oils for automobiles and all types of machines. The typical temperature range is 480–750°F (250–400°C).
- Near the base of the tower, it is 660–930°F (350–500°C). The fractions collecting here are heavy gas or fuel oils used in industry, and for changing into other products.
- In the base of the tower are the residuals—asphalt (or bitumen), tars, and waxes. The temperature down here is usually over 930°F (500°C).

Cracking and Alkylation

The tall fractionation column may not be the end of the refining story. Some of the fractions can, in effect, be changed into others by processes such as cracking and alkylation.

Cracking changes heavier fractions into lighter ones. For example, in fluid **catalytic** cracking, the oil faction is heated until it vaporizes, and then it's mixed with tiny particles of a chemical catalyst. The two substances swirl around almost like a fluid (hence the name), usually at more than 930°F (500°C). The catalyst helps the large molecules of the fraction to break into smaller ones. The oil vapors go to a fractionation tower, as described above, while the used catalyst is heated and "cleaned" so it can be used again. A second method is thermal or steam cracking, which uses extreme heat and pressure to break apart the molecules in a similar way.

Alkylation is another chemical process at the refinery. In one sense, this is the opposite of cracking. Alkylation uses chemical catalysts to join together small molecules from light fractions to make bigger, heavier ones.

In this way, the refinery can respond to the types of crude it receives and the demand for its products. For instance, if heavy oil is not needed urgently, it can be cracked to make gasoline. The naptha fraction can be cracked to give substances like propene and ethylene, which are used to make plastics.

Smooth Roads

One of the heaviest oil fractions—bitumen, or asphalt—makes the modern world run smoothly. Heated until it is runny, and mixed with small stones or gravel called ballast, it works like a glue or binder. Rolled flat, it sets hard and smooth to cover our sidewalks, streets, and highways.

TEXT-DEPENDENT QUESTIONS

1. What does API gravity measure?
2. What are the average temperatures at the top and bottom of a fractionation tower?
3. Which process joins together molecules of an oil fraction to make them heavier, and which breaks them apart to become lighter?

RESEARCH PROJECTS

1. Find out how the amounts of sulfur in crude oil affect its refining. Which is more useful, sweet or sour crude?
2. Research the two main types of cracking, fluid catalyst and steam/thermal. Which came first and which is most popular today?

Chapter Four

THE OIL INDUSTRY

The 1859 Drake Well in Pennsylvania (see page 20) was the first to make people realize that oil could become a big industry. Other wells were soon drilled in the area. The "Pennsylvanian oil rush" took hold, although it only lasted a few decades. Oil prospectors, known as wildcatters, continued to search across the nation, with only minor luck until they came to Oklahoma, then Texas and other states bordering the Gulf of Mexico. In 1894, drillers looking for water found a large oilfield by chance near Corsicana, Texas. This attracted many others to the area, and wells sprang up in hundreds of locations.

Words to Understand

monopoly: when one company or corporation is much larger than others in its area of business, with too much power for fair competition.

revenue: money coming in from selling products or services.

sustainable: a resource or process that can continue for the foreseeable future, rather than running out of resources or other needs.

A gusher near Beaumont, Texas, photographed in 1901.

By 1900 the oil industry was also growing in Europe, Russia, and Central Asia. The Russian Empire, with territories such as modern Azerbaijan, was the world's leading producer. Then, in 1901, the Spindletop gusher near Beaumont, Texas, launched large-scale US oil production, as described in the next chapter. The drillers, led by the oil expert Captain Anthony F. Lucas, hoped the well might yield 5 to 10 barrels (roughly 800 to 1600 liters) daily. It soon became clear it was more like 100,000 barrels each day—more than all other US oil wells of the time added together. The Texas oil boom and the modern "Age of Oil" had begun.

In the meantime, automobiles, invented back in 1879, were spreading. Demand grew for gasoline fuel. The first roadside gas pumps in the United States were installed in 1885 in Fort Wayne, Indiana. The Texas oil boom made gasoline fuel more widespread. Then, in 1908, Henry Ford introduced his Model T. Soon, many more people could buy autos, and the demand for gasoline grew larger. In addition, dirt roads were being surfaced with smooth asphalt, another oil product. In a spiral of growth, oil was the new "black gold."

Oil Companies

The first big US oil company was Standard Oil of Ohio, founded in 1870 by a group of business and industry leaders led by John D Rockefeller. The company grew fast but used methods that many people disliked, such as bullying competitors, or buying them up and closing them down. By the 1880s, the Standard Oil Company had begun transporting oil long distances, in North America and then, as the first multinational oil company, across Europe and around the world. It found new inventions and markets for oil products once thrown away as waste.

By 1900, Standard Oil controlled nine-tenths of all oil production in the United States. But its methods were being investigated. It was accused of being a monopoly—a business so big that it could do what it liked, make secret agreements with suppliers and sellers, destroy competitors, and keep prices high.

Petroleum Jelly

On the early Pennsylvania oil rigs, in about 1860, drillers were annoyed by a waxy substance that caused problems with the machinery. However, when smeared on burns and cuts, it reduced pain and helped healing. The chemist Robert Chesebrough purified the wax into a a new product called petroleum jelly and began selling it in 1870. We now know Chesebrough's product as Vaseline.

John D. Rockefeller, left, with his son, John D. Rockefeller, Jr., in 1915.

In 1911 the US Supreme Court ordered Standard Oil to be broken up into more than 30 smaller, separate companies. One was the Standard Oil Company of New Jersey, which would later become Exxon. Another was the Standard Oil Company of New York, or Socony. This changed to Socony–Vacuum in 1931, Socony Mobil Oil Company in 1955, and Mobil in 1966. Then in 1998–1999, Mobil joined back with Exxon to form ExxonMobil. This is only one example of how complicated the oil industry can be, with its many breakups, mergers, and parent companies.

Oil around the World

By 1950, the United States was producing about half of the world's oil. However, production was also growing in the Middle East, and also in Mexico and South America, especially in Venezuela. Russia, too, was increasing production fast. American demand for oil grew faster than the nation could supply, so it began to import oil from other regions, especially the Middle East.

The Top Ten Oil-Consuming Nations

1. United States
2. China
3. Japan
4. India
5. Russia
6. Brazil
7. Saudi Arabia
8. Germany
9. South Korea
10. Canada

The 1970s saw two major energy crises. These were partly due to political and military problems. Two major examples were the

The Trans-Alaska pipeline.

Yom Kippur War (also called the Arab-Israeli War) in 1973, and the Islamic Revolution in Iran in 1979. Oil prices multiplied several times in response to these events. As prices rose, some people began to question society's dependence on gasoline, heating oil, industrial oils, and other petroleum products. Meanwhile, the potentially harmful effects of oil products on the environment were becoming more clear. People also began to realize the limited nature of oil reserves. This started a movement toward less polluting, more **sustainable** ways of obtaining and using energy.

Today, in terms of **revenue**, seven of the world's top ten companies are in the oil and gas business. North America no longer has the biggest oil companies. But its petroleum businesses retain great power in today's global market, with transport of crude oil around the world, and links to the transport, chemical, and other industries. New oilfields are being developed from Alaska to the Gulf of Mexico, even though the cost of finding oil rises all the time—on average, nine out of ten boreholes exploring a new region are "dry."

Recently, in a great about-turn, the increase in horizontal drilling and fracking has allowed the United States to reduce oil imports significantly. By 2014, it was once again the world's leading oil producer, taking over from Saudi Arabia and Russia. This not only secures North America's petroleum supplies for many years, but it also means the United States and Canada depend less on oil from other countries. Some experts hope this will mean they are less affected by political problems and military conflicts around the world.

Top Ten Oil-Producing Companies

1. Saudi Aramco: 12.5 million barrels per day
2. Gazprom: 9.7 million barrels per day
3. National Iranian Oil Company: 6.4 million barrels per day
4. ExxonMobil: 5.3 million barrels per day (US-based)
5. PetroChina: 4.4 million barrels per day
6. BP: 4.1 million barrels per day
7. Royal Dutch Shell: 3.9 million barrels per day
8. Pemex: 3.6 million barrels per day
9. Chevron: 3.5 million barrels per day (US-based)
10. Kuwait Petroleum Corporation: 3.2 million barrels per day

TEXT-DEPENDENT QUESTIONS

1. How did the spread of the automobile influence the oil industry?
2. Which two companies that came from the breakup of Standard Oil got together again in 1998–1999?
3. What kinds of problems caused the 1970s energy crises?

RESEARCH PROJECTS

1. Find out more about Standard Oil's monopoly, and about the breakup of the company. What does antitrust mean, and have such laws been strengthened since?
2. Research some products that were invented to make use of oil industry "waste," such as Vaseline.
3. Which countries use the most oil per person? There are some small nations where the average consumption of oil for each individual is twice as much as in the United States.

Chapter Five

OIL AND THE ENVIRONMENT

The world's first well-known gusher, or oil blowout, was a Lucas well at the Spindletop site in Beaumont, Texas, in January 1901 (see above, page 40). From a depth of 1,150 feet (350 meters), oil at massive pressure blasted up the borehole more than 150 feet (46 meters) into the air for over one week. An estimated half-million barrels of oil flooded over the ground. Some was collected in a "lake" and scooped up. But most local people, far from being worried at the pollution, were overjoyed that their area was rich in oil. The Texas oil boom followed, with money and power pouring into the state as the oil poured out.

The Spindletop gusher, and similar accidents, eventually led to improvements such as blowout preventers. As the oil boom continued, however, what had been small-scale problems grew bigger. Also, as more nations became oil producers, these problems spread around the world. And as the general public grew more aware about dangers to the environment, the oil industry became a favorite media villain. At the same time, oil can be seen as an easy target. It is such a giant industry, with vast profits and massive publicity, that it is easy to criticize and protest against—even though, every day, its protesters and critics rely on its products.

There are certainly many environmental concerns associated with the production and use of oil. The presence of onshore oil rigs, platforms, pumps, refineries, and storage can ruin huge areas of natural scenery. Offshore rigs are at risk from storms,

Oil companies are frequent targets of environmental protests, such as this anti-fracking demonstration in California in 2014.

fires, and similar accidents. Leaks, pollution, and explosions are ever-present hazards. Transporting oil and its products is so common that, like any other way of moving cargo, accidents are almost certain to occur. Three recent North American incidents—each at a different point along oil's journey from well to tanker to refinery—highlight the terrible dangers that still occur.

Extraction: *Deepwater Horizon* (2010)

In April 2010, the world was gripped by news of a major oil spill in the Gulf of Mexico. It occurred at the offshore BP *Deepwater Horizon* oil rig located about

After the *Deepwater Horizon* disaster, crews burn off some of the oil floating in the Gulf of Mexico.

40 miles (64 kilometers) from the coast of Louisiana, near New Orleans. The rig was floating and secured in position in water about 5,100 feet (1,500 meters) deep. It was drilling an exploratory borehole that went 13,200 feet (4,020 meters), or 2.5 miles (4 kilometers), into the seabed. At around 9:45 a.m. on April 20, methane gas from far below came up the well into the rig itself and exploded. Of the 126 crew members on board, 11 were killed and 17 were injured. The rig burned for two days, and then slipped under the waves.

On the afternoon that the rig sank, a floating oil layer, or slick, formed on the ocean. Its size and growth showed that crude oil was leaking from the wellhead on the seabed below at the rate of up to 60,000 barrels per day. Over the following weeks, numerous attempts were made

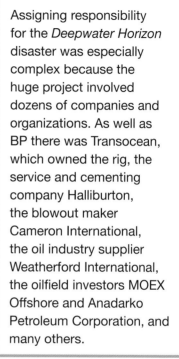

A Tangled Web

Assigning responsibility for the *Deepwater Horizon* disaster was especially complex because the huge project involved dozens of companies and organizations. As well as BP there was Transocean, which owned the rig, the service and cementing company Halliburton, the blowout maker Cameron International, the oil industry supplier Weatherford International, the oilfield investors MOEX Offshore and Anadarko Petroleum Corporation, and many others.

to stop the underwater gusher. The blowout was finally stopped, and the well "died" in September, after almost 13 weeks and nearly 5 million leaked barrels of oil.

The oil slick spread over a vast area of the Gulf and lapped ashore on the coastline. Attempts were made to limit the terrible environmental damage. Chemicals called dispersants were used to break up the oil into tiny globules that would hopefully cause less harm—but some experts said this method caused even worse problems. Other methods were tried, including setting fire to the slick in controlled ways, and collecting the oil–water mix to remove the oil. Hundreds of miles of floating barriers called containment booms tried to stop the oil reaching the shore. Nonetheless, seabirds, fish, and other ocean life were devastated. Long stretches of coastline were polluted, from Texas to Florida, affecting leisure resorts; scenic areas; fisheries for crab, shrimp, and shellfish; and the livelihoods of thousands of people.

A long investigation identified several problems that combined to cause the disaster. They included pipes not being properly positioned in the center of the

A pelican covered in oil after the *Deepwater Horizon* spill.

borehole, problems with "mud" flow and cement for the casings, lack of attention to pressure tests, and poor maintenance of the blowout preventer. Lengthy court cases followed against BP and other companies. Clean-up costs, fines, and other money matters have been estimated at more than $40 billion.

Transportation: *Exxon Valdez* (1989)

After extraction, the next stage of oil's journey is transportation. In March 1989, the 200,000-ton tanker *Exxon Valdez* was sailing from the oil terminal port of Valdez, Alaska, to Long Beach, California. In Prince William Sound, about 25 miles (40 kilometers) from Valdez, it ran onto a shallow rocky area known as Bligh Reef. The ship split open, and over the following days it leaked at least one-fifth of its load—about 250,000 barrels, but possibly much more—into the surrounding waters. The suffocating, polluting layer spread to cover more than 10,000 square miles (26,000 square kilometers) of ocean and wash up on 1,500 miles (2,400 kilometers) of shoreline.

As with *Deepwater Horizon*, several factors led to the *Exxon Valdez* oil spill. Apparently the ship's radar system, which should warn of collision, was out of order. The crew were working long hours without enough rest, especially as they rushed to leave Valdez, being late on their schedule. The tanker was not on its usual route due to iceberg warnings. And at the controls was the third mate, rather than the captain or another senior, experienced person. (The captain, Joseph Hazelwood, was eventually convicted of negligence.)

The oil spill brought enormous damage to this wild and beautiful part of North America. Global television carried pictures of dying, oil-soaked seabirds. Many other

Both Navy and civilian crews worked to clean up the *Exxon Valdez* spill in 1989.

well-known animals were affected, from bald eagles to sea otters, killer whales, harbor seals, and huge numbers of fish and small sea life. The food webs and ecology of the region were destroyed.

Clean-up attempts included chemical dispersants, explosions and burning, containment booms, and skimmers to lift away the oil. Birds and other animals were treated, and oil on the shore was blasted with high-pressure hot water and steam to break it up. However, these measures were too little, too late. Unlike the warmer conditions of the Gulf, in this cold region the oil stayed thick and sticky, and its natural process of breaking down, called biodegradation, was extremely slow. Surveys 25 years later showed thousands of gallons of oil remained along the coast, some of it having drifted more than 400 miles (64 kilometers).

Refinery: The Texas City Explosion (2005)

Crude oil's journey ends at the refinery, where it is separated into its many fractions. In March 2005, there was a huge explosion at the Texas City Refinery, on the state's Gulf coast. This city is known for an even more massive explosion that occurred back in 1947 (see sidebar). The 2005 event occurred when vapors leaked from an overflow in one of the towers, and were sparked into blowing up, probably by an automobile engine.

The 1947 Texas City Disaster

Oil was involved in the worst loss of life in any North American industrial accident. In 1947, a ship carrying chemicals exploded in the Texas City port, setting off a series of further explosions and fires in other ships, and in oil storage tanks and warehouses along the shore. Over 580 people died and large areas of the city were destroyed.

As with the *Deepwater Horizon* and *Exxon Valdez* disasters, many things contributed to the tragedy, including ill-advised measures to cut costs, poor working procedures, failures in management, poor training, lack of attention to safety, alarms and sensors that did not work, vehicles too close to hazards, and old, outdated, and faulty equipment.

The Texas City Refinery explosion did little environmental damage, since it was on a huge industrial site. However, the human cost

Easy Targets?

In addition to environmental concerns, another big challenge for the oil industry involves the potential for sabotage and terrorism. Oil wells, tanker vessels, pipelines, refineries, and oil storage depots have been "soft targets" for those using violence to further their cause. In 2014, for example, several important oil refineries in Iraq were seized by Islamic State (ISIS) forces, and then bombed by US-led coalition air attacks. North America has not so far suffered any significant attacks, but security experts keep a wary eye on the potential for destruction.

Men working at a refinery in Baghdad, Iraq. Many believe that refineries are at high risk from terrorist attack.

was extremely high: 15 people lost their lives, and another 180 were injured. As with the other disasters, oil companies said they would learn lessons and improve their safety record.

Supporters of the oil business point out that accidents happen, and that lives are lost in many other industries and activities, from modern agriculture and chemical production to simply driving on the highway. However these events

The petrochemical industry makes our modern lifestyle possible, but it brings with it many environmental risks.

rarely have the huge environmental impact of an oil spill, partly because oil flows and burns.

Positives and Negatives

Burning fossil fuels has an enormous impact on the environment. It is a massive cause of smog and associated air pollution. Carbon dioxide produced by any form of burning is a powerful greenhouse gas, making Earth gradually heat up, which is known as global warming—and this is leading to climate change. Burning gasoline and other fuels made from oil contributes some two-fifths of all US carbon dioxide emissions. Oil supporters might argue that the industry is simply supplying demand and giving consumers what they want. Consumers could opt out by not running gas-powered vehicles, not using power from fossil fuel sources, and avoiding plastics, paints, and many other everyday items made from oil. But is that realistic?

The rapid growth of fracking in North America poses new environmental concerns. Since it is comparatively recent, its long-term effects are not yet known. Fracking sites include big storage tanks and other facilities that could damage and leak. The chemicals can escape and contaminate soil, **groundwater,** or surface water around the location. Also, fracking fluid pumped into the rocks might spread and contaminate groundwater, soil, plants, and animals from below. There are even worries that fracking could disturb deep rocks enough to lead to earth tremors. These concerns have led many people to oppose the practice, and it has been banned by some towns and cities. (This topic is discussed in more detail in the *Natural Gas* title of this series.)

In today's world, oil is being used up billions of times faster than it was made. Reserves of this most precious resource will dwindle, threatening our whole modern way of life. This would be especially serious in the developed region of North America, with its high oil use and generally well-off lifestyles. It may not happen for another hundred years. But effects on the environment, from a local pollution leak to worldwide climate change, are here and now.

TEXT-DEPENDENT QUESTIONS

1. Identify similarities among the causes of the *Deepwater Horizon*, *Exxon Valdez*, and Texas City Refinery disasters.
2. What are some of the methods used to clean up an oil spill?
3. What are three possible hazards from fracking?

RESEARCH PROJECTS

1. Find out about the world's biggest oil spills. Where do the United States and Canada stand on the list?
2. Look into how much of global warming is due to burning oil as a fuel. What are the alternatives?

Further Reading

BOOKS

Doeden, Matt. *Finding Out about Coal, Oil, and Natural Gas.* Searchlight Books: What Are Energy Sources? Minneapolis, MN: Lerner Publications, 2014.

Farndon, John. *Oil.* Rev. ed. DK Eyewitness Books. New York: Dorling Kindersley, 2012.

Horn, Geoffrey M., and Debra Voege. *Coal, Oil, and Natural Gas, (Energy Today).* New York: Chelsea House, 2010.

Marcovitz, Hal. *What Is the Future of Fossil Fuels? Future of Renewable Energy.* San Diego, CA: ReferencePoint Press, 2013.

Nelson, Drew. *Life on an Oil Rig. Extreme Jobs in Extreme Places.* New York: Gareth Stevens, 2013.

Simon, Seymour. *Global Warming.* New York: HarperCollins, 2013.

ONLINE

Alberta Energy. "About Oil." http://www.energy.alberta.ca/Oil/574.asp.

American Petroleum Institute. "Oil and Natural Gas Overview." http://www.api.org/oil-and-natural-gas-overview.

Energy Kids. "Oil (Petroleum) Basics." US Energy Information Administration. http://www.eia.gov/kids/energy.cfm?page=oil_home-basics.

Series Glossary

alloy: mixture of two or more metals.

alluvial: relating to soil that is deposited by running water.

aquicludes: layers of rocks through which groundwater cannot flow.

aquifer: an underground water source.

archeologists: scientists who study ancient cultures by examining their material remains, such as buildings, tools, and other artifacts.

biodegradable: the process by which bacteria and organisms naturally break down a substance.

biodiversity: the variety of life; all the living things in an area, or on Earth on the whole.

by-product: a substance or material that is not the main desired product of a process but happens to be made along the way.

carbon: a pure chemical substance or element, symbol C, found in great amounts in living and once-living things.

catalyst: a substance that speeds up a chemical change or reaction that would otherwise happen slowly, if at all.

commodity: an item that is bought and sold.

compound: two or more elements chemically bound together.

constituent: ingredient; one of the parts of a whole.

contaminated: polluted with harmful substances.

convection: circular motion of a liquid or gas resulting from temperature differences.

corrosion: the slow destruction of metal by various chemical processes.

dredge: a machine that can remove material from under water.

emissions: substances given off by burning or similar chemical changes.

excavator: a machine, usually with one or more toothed wheels or buckets that digs material out of the ground.

flue gases: gases produced by burning and other processes that come out of flues, stacks, chimneys, and similar outlets.

forges: makes or shapes metal by heating it in furnaces or beating or hammering it.

fossil fuels: sources of fuel, such as oil and coal, that contain carbon and come from the decomposed remains of prehistoric plants and animals.

fracking: shorthand for hydraulic fracturing, a method of extracting gas and oil from rocks.

fusion: energy generated by joining two or more atoms.

geologists: scientists who study Earth's structure or that of another planet.

greenhouse gas: a gas that helps to trap and hold heat—much like the panes of glass in a greenhouse.

hydrocarbon: a substance containing only the pure chemical substances, or elements, carbon and hydrogen.

hydrologic cycle: events in which water vapor condenses and falls to the surface as rain, snow, or sleet, and then evaporates and returns to the atmosphere.

indigenous: growing or living naturally in a particular region or environment.

inorganic: compound of minerals rather than living material.

kerogens: a variety of substances formed when once-living things decayed and broke down, on the way to becoming natural gas or oil.

leachate: liquid containing wastes.

mineralogists: scientists who study minerals and how to classify, locate, and distinguish them.

nonrenewable resources: natural resources that are not replenished over time; these exist in fixed, limited supplies.

ore: naturally occurring mineral from which metal can be extracted.

ozone: a form of oxygen containing three atoms of oxygen in a molecule.

porous: allowing a liquid to seep or soak through small holes and channels.

primordial: existing at the beginning of time.

producer gas: a gas created ("produced") by industrial rather than natural means.

reclamation: returning something to its former state.

reducing agent: a substance that decreases another substance in a chemical reaction.

refine: to make something purer, or separate it into its various parts.

remote sensing: detecting and gathering information from a distance, for example, when satellites in space measure air and ground temperature below.

renewable: a substance that can be made, or a process used, again and again.

reserves: amounts in store, which can be used in the future.

runoff: water not absorbed by the soil that flows into lakes, streams, rivers, and oceans.

seismology: the study of waves, as vibrations or "shaking," that pass through the Earth's rocks, soils, and other structures.

sequestration: storing or taking something to keep it for a time.

shaft: a vertical passage that gives miners access to mine.

sluice: artificial water channel that is controlled by a value or gate.

slurry: a mixture of water and a solid that can't be dissolved.

smelting: the act of separating metal from rock by melting it at high temperatures

subsidence: the sinking down of land resulting from natural shifts or human activities.

sustainable: able to carry on for a very long time, at least the foreseeable future.

synthesis: making or producing something by adding substances together.

tailing: the waste product left over after ore has been extracted from rock.

tectonic: relating to the structure and movement of the earth's crust.

watercourse: a channel along which water flows, such as a brook, creek, or river.

Index

(page numbers in *italics* refer to photographs and illustrations)

About the Author

Steve Parker is an author and editor of children's non-fiction books and websites, chiefly in the areas of nature and the biological sciences. He has written more than 100 titles about the natural world, animals and plants, ecology, conservation, rocks and fossils, mineral wealth, and Earth's varied and valuable resources—and how human activities are affecting them, both historically and into the future. Steve's recent works include the *Animal Diaries* series (QED, London) about how our exploitation of land, water, air and the general environment affects the daily lives of creatures as diverse as a garden spider, lion, penguin, golden eagle and shark.

Photo Credits

Cover

Clockwise from left: Dollar Photo Club/eyeidea; Dollar Photo Club/gemenacom; Dollar Photo Club/Ded Pixto; iStock.com/predrag1; Dollar Photo Club/tashatuvango; Dollar Photo Club/Minerva Studio; Dollar Photo Club/smereka

Interior

British Library: 31.

Dollar Photo Club: 11 kojihirano; 14 sframe; 36 Steve Mann; 37 RAW; 41 WavebreakMediaMicro.

iStock.com: 12 itakefotos4u; 22 ahopueo; 23 mikeuk; 28 wesvandinter; 33 albertogagna; 35 AlbanyPictures; 43 urbanraven; 47 DnHolm; 53 EdStock; 54 TomasSereda.

Library of Congress: 15 Carol M. Highsmith; 40; 42.

Wikimedia Commons: 19 Abraham Cresques; 20 Thaddeus Mortimer Fowler; 24 BoH; 26 Joshua Doubek; 48 Justin Stumberg; 50 Louisiana GOHSEP; 51 PH2 POCHE.